AS LONG AS YOU'RE HAPPY

As Long As You're Happy

POEMS BY

JACK
MYERS

GRAYWOLF PRESS · SAINT PAUL

ACKNOWLEDGMENTS

Some of these poems have appeared previously in *Cedar Rock, The Chowder Review, Crazy Horse, Fiction International, The Great River Review, Missouri Review, North American Review, The Ohio Review, Pacific Review, Telescope, Tendril, Virginia Quarterly Review* and *The Wooster Review.*

"The Diaspora" appeared in *The Ohio Review Ten-Year Retrospective,* 1983.

"A Manner of Speaking," "Coming to the Surface," "As Long as You're Happy," "The Diaspora," "Do You Know What I Mean?" and "Natural Ice Cream" appeared in *New American Poets of the 80s,* an anthology from Wampeter Press, 1984.

A number of the poems in this book were previously published in *Coming to the Surface,* a chapbook from Trilobite Press, 1984.

The author wishes to thank the National Endowment for the Arts, whose Fellowship helped make a number of these poems possible.

Publication of this volume is made possible in part by a grant from the National Endowment for the Arts, and in part by generous contributions to Graywolf Press from individuals, corporations and foundations.

Published by GRAYWOLF PRESS
Post Office Box 75006
Saint Paul, Minnesota 55175

The National Poetry Series was established in 1978 to publish five collections of poetry annually through five participating publishers. The manuscripts are selected by five poets of national reputation. Publication is funded by James A. Michener, Edward J. Piszek, The Ford Foundation, The Mobil Foundation, Exxon Corporation, The National Endowment for the Arts, The Friends of the National Poetry Series and the five publishers — E. P. Dutton, Graywolf Press, William Morrow & Co., Persea Books, and The University of Illinois Press.

1985

LOCAL TIME

Stephen Dunn
Selected by Dave Smith / William Morrow & Co.

PALLADIUM

Alice Fulton
Selected by Mark Strand / University of Illinois Press

SAINTS

Reginald Gibbons
Selected by Roland Flint / Persea Books

AS LONG AS YOU'RE HAPPY

Jack Myers
Selected by Seamus Heaney / Graywolf Press

LIVING GLOVES

Lynn Doyle
Selected by Cynthia MacDonald / E. P. Dutton

FOR WILLA

CONTENTS

1. Something Solid

2. The Diamond Explanation

3. The Diaspora

1

Something

Solid

Being arches itself   over the vast abyss.
Ah the ball that we dared,   that we hurled into infinite space,
doesn't it fill our hands   differently with its return:
heavier by the weight   of where it has been

— Rainer Maria Rilke

Something Solid

First thing in the morning
I open my eyes,
look into the mirror
of my old armoire,
a bald man in stolen hospital pajamas
expecting to see
a distinguished man of letters,
like when the wine steward
stands over you
and expects you to decide
if what's in your mouth
meets the test
of whether the last ten years
in darkness
were good or not,

only this time
the door is open
and I'm staring incomprehensibly at five shelves
glutted with colored clothes:
"Wow, it's like looking inside my head!"
And then I think with these rags-for-brains
like the Straw Man does in *Oz*
about the whole idea of wearing clothes
and how beautifully my wife gets dressed
and how petty bourgeoisie materialism
turns out to be pretty smart,

when about this time
Mr. Pernell, retired oilman and rancher,
marches by the house on his morning exercise

with his wife walking ten yards behind him
as if they don't know each other
and he's thinking to himself,
"This is Professor Myers' house,"
and he's feeling good about the neighborhood
whose citizens, like me, he thinks,
have achieved something solid.

Arf

Dogs give commands to me in one syllable,
the same one again and again.
I speak back in polysyllabics
above my one great bark.

It's like my dreams falling all night
in technicolor splendor. I can't remember what.
When I open my eyes and look back
I'm just grateful I fit my body through
this space as big as a bark.

And the conversations I have with myself each day....
They're like those silver balls on poles
across which gags of burnt electricity arc.
And I'm laid out below, inert,
until my head smokes and I stagger off
with a grunt-thought, cough-out, my smashed send-off.

The same thing happened to my friend Larry
who claims he never woke up at birth.
So for $45 the holistic doctor placed a
bouillon cube on his forehead and a lump
of cheese over his heart, and Larry woke up
and coughed and coughed in dog language
and we knew to bring him water. It was a miracle!
Only we're not sure what.

I imagine that's why we have the public flasher
who is able to prepare us
for the right moment on some random day
when he'll drop the blinding light of his body

down in front of us: "Bark!"
He makes us feel exact.

My intuition tells me yes
even a stone can bark.
Only the sound it makes is millions of years long
and I'm standing in the silence and dark
between its two great phonemes of need,
going to sleep, waking up, going to sleep.

Do You Know What I Mean

For the sake of argument
let's say there are three of me:
the one with the bummed-out body,
the one who senses things are going badly,
and the bright one who can't cope. That's me!
Don't get me wrong. It's a family.
For example, if #2 has a sexy dream,
#1 may salivate. That leaves 3 free to feel guilty
or write. Only sometimes in the face of authority
1 opens his mouth and 3 slips out "I hate your guts!"
Then 2 tries to get 3 to repent, but isn't smart enough
and then everyone feels like shit and gets a headache.

Do you know what I mean?

2 and 3 are always sniffing each other suspiciously
while 1 sticks a bottle of sour mash in his face.
We know that somewhere some elegant in a gray silk suit
and shiny black shoes reflecting the tips of the Alps
is slowly turning toward his tasty companion
the date 1957 on their green bottle of pouille-fuissé.

I did that so #3 would feel better
having said a spot of French.
That means 1 has the green light to celebrate
and 2 can slink around pretending he's French.

*

Dear God,
I don't believe in you,
but #2 is feeling bad today.
He thinks you're out there and you're great.
But he can't tell the difference between something small
tearing apart and the sound of something large in the distance
moving far off.

So this is for my brother, #2,
standing here like we're in church.
Sometimes when we're quiet like this
I think we're all the family we've got.

Day Off: Tangle Thinks

Everything on this random day
comes down to whether I squint or gape.
This must be the disease my grandmother had for years,
the blue of an injured fingernail moving through her body,
through the phone until it is the dark awareness shining
from my head.

I have medicines for calming organs, loosening muscles,
and some appliances that heat or freeze me.

I have tools for hitting, tools for holding,
and something for getting inside.

*

After another long day I lie down exhausted
beside my box of Decorated Facial Tissues.

Someone has printed a garden of pink roses
for me to blow my nose in. Good.

I imagine the tulips in their dank bathrooms
have rolls of toilet paper with repeating human heads.

In the backyard next door, toddlers keep bumping into one another
despite their bright clothing and little beeps.

I am the bald man next door
who is always under control.

What if I crawled around with them
and ate their lunch
of black sticks and muck,
and we all beat against our messy laps
and just went crazy?

Then what?

Headache

I tried to remember to buy aspirin and soap
but I only bought the aspirin.
I liked the way that worked, the way I made my choice
unbeknownst to me. It was clean, as if I knew something
way down deep.

Because what if I only bought the soap?
Then I'd be locked out of my head in pain
trying to reach my brain by transcendental meditation,
which only makes the pain more real.

On the other hand, what if I bought both,
which may be normal;
what if I remembered everything?

No thanks, I want to know who's on first.
I want my mind made up even if it means
I don't feel normal, or I have to keep a list,
which reminds me

of my delivery bike which George Lynch stole
and then he sold it and I got fired and then
he moved away. He is no more to me
than the window of light shining on that apple seed.
Besides, I'd rather be right than clean,
the little prick.

Where I've Been

At last I am ready to report
how so much of my time
has been spent lost between
thinking and feeling

that seen from above
it must look like a river
cutting its way between
age and circumstance
leaving behind something wet
and abstract as the insides of a jewel.

How I came to accept this habit
after wiping these journeys out
like dirty thoughts, pronouncing myself
time after time as being lost
is a testament to whatever lies
beyond my will.

I can hardly look at anything
as complex and frightening
as the human face, its ability to imagine
moving inward
at such tremendous speeds
it outruns the Postmaster's fear
of having to read his jumbled horde of letters.

All this is to my shame, my chandelier
of egotism burning in an empty head.
I feel as archaic as a candelabrum
floating in outer space.
I have even stopped writing poetry
thinking a simple report will do.

Planting Stones

I picked up a 25-pound rock
walked into the ocean chest-high
then sat down.

I thought the flaws within
might float away
like splinters.

I thought of walking toward Europe
and bursting on the horizon
like a great idea.

In the end there was an acre
of wall-sized stones, each one
solid as a held breath,
each one a moment to myself.

Coming to the Surface

Sometimes you get tired of the dark, the humming,
the shimmering, and the echoes of others,
the whole long story that robs you of your life.

So you break into the world
of air and light
just to feel heavy and freezing,
which is a good release from thinking
but not a permanent cure.

Once in a while someone plunges by you
with his whole being combed back
into a scream of forgetfulness,
a command.

He's going the other way.

Synchronization

What was I thinking
when they allowed me to choose
from all the orchards of music
and I picked the accordian?

I was thinking of my fierce brother
falling through ice and blackness
trying to master the piano
while with one finger I thought
I could make a piano rise from the sea.

What was I thinking
when I modeled my best moment after
a bird startled into flight?

I was thinking of the sky
lowered to my height
so I could fly at eye level.

What I wanted was both sides fused
like the face of a one-eyed Jack,
to go out in ermine with a faceful
of triumphal bugles.

And if that brightened the air
and burned the tips of leaves a little,
well, that's life.

What I didn't want was to go out searching
for the usual spicule of insight.
All I wanted was to go out thinking
I did what I thought I said.

Elsewhere

Sitting at a checkered tablecloth
listening to myself breathe,
I feel like the man who invented
the boredom of accordian music.

I would like to compose
an image of my life
whose sheer weight
is quiet enough
to last a lifetime.

But to be alone like this
shakes the blossoms
from the stick trees
again and again.

I think how grief exactly fits
the size of anything living,
how it's infinitely expandable,

but I am no more than a mote
floating through the small blue sky
of someone's mind, darkening
his rights and privileges.

Knowing this, I am lifted up
and then there is a calm, a settlement
of white blossoms,
trees like massive nerves
holding up the sky.

Feeling My Way

When I woke up to this life
like a scream trying to empty itself out
they couldn't put their arms around my anger.

Born too soon, even the details of the leaves
wouldn't let me breathe. Then I learned
how God chose me to wear a skullcap

like a bad child, and I put my face into my hands –
the only thing I ever invented – which came to pass
for a lifetime of long thought. It was there

I heard the very hum and wheel of myself turn
which I turned into my religion. Finally I was in charge.
Then one day I spied a woman, head in hands,

who sat listening to herself. Kindness lifted her face
and we had many children who said the things that took me
all my life to learn. Who doesn't want to start over

with one tooth, a little candle, and long hours of sleep?
But then will come the scream. Then again, like the blindman
feeling his way up an elephant's leg until all he imagines

is a skyful of leaves, maybe only half of this is true.

Poem against Good Health

I quit all my bad habits so I could grow old
and one day say something big enough
to climb into and close like a box.

That's how one year went up in smoke,
waiting for whatever I did smart
to harden into words
while the nothing behind me
and the nothing before me
marched forward in their place.

All my consciousness
focused on what was different
so I forgot the main thing
like when you spot a fly in the room
the whole room softens and disappears.

I became what I wanted to change.

Now it's impossible even to be simple,
but I've added years to my life
which is as invisible as if it never existed
and everyone's so proud of me.

I Already Tried Gardening…

I was digging the borderline garden I had conceived of
in a flash and analyzed all winter, clumps of black clay
fastened with grass, which became forced labor so I worked
harder hoping when I looked up it'd all have turned to flowers.

Just as robins migrating from Mexico had reached Dallas,
an old man with a battle-axe cane stopped by and said, "I can't
figure what you're doing." Looking through his glasses I could see
his house clear across the street. "And what denomination are you?"
he asked. So then I knew where I lived and I backed him up with
"God told me to do it. It's artistic."

Then he asked, "What are ya gonna do with them piles of good dirt?"
It was disguised as a craft question, and I thought he could've been
one of those Old Masters who can hyperspace when cornered, so I said
"I'm digging a hole in the hill and moving it out back."

He noticed how the hole was smaller than the hill and said, "Holes
get bigger more slowly than hills. You're welcome to attend
our church." I said, "See that cane? I call it your tree-leg."
He said, "I'm bird-brain and this here dog you don't see which is
home I call 'Leave.'" Then I got on my knees and said to my work,

"But don't make me eat one of those delicious clumps of chocolate-
pudding dirt," which I mashed with my feet and I did my karate yells
like Shredded Wheat amplified a hundred times and the robins jumped
into the bare plum tree and argued about who's the boss and who'll
get the best-looking women while that old man stared at me,

both of us not knowing my denomination, and the question of the birds
in the air: Should we camp here tonight?

The Correspondence School Poetry Teacher Speaks on the Relationship between Life and Art

They send me poems
like gargantuan emeralds
crashed into my house,

huge sputters of
wetness and light.

I, who, according to the best of my knowledge,
may or may not
have my socks on,

who can't remember how to call home
in cases of emergency,
they send me poems.

I forget the reasons why this reminds me
that our heads are
so disproportionately large at birth,

but I'll share with you instead
my basic principle:
"If you're thirsty, think of sour pickles."

I even have a slogan for the heart:
"Redeem yourself. Wipe out memory!"
No memory, no life, no art.

I have worked my way back down
to exactly what I've become —
vicarious, the ideal reader.

As Uncle Irv who sold storm windows used to say
when he'd wake up from his nap on Sunday visits,
"What...?"

Self-Addressed Trains of Thought

– in memory of my memory

Once, I wrote down a thought
and mailed it to myself
so it would have importance and surprise.

I didn't write "Dear Jack" or "Best wishes."
I said to myself, "Imagine when this arrives
how it will intersect with some future thought!"

I scared myself a little
with my misunderstanding of the phrase "future thought."
But that's exactly what would happen. Something innocuous
but extraordinary, something dangerous but ordinary
would land in my life, and I would finally be at both ends.

Then I'd get up from this life
and estimate the situation.

Dog-Eat-Dog World

My boss called out of the blue today
wondering why I haven't been to work
which reminds me of the time I was staring at the wall
and a little black head with a pair of antennae
broke through and I drenched it in bug spray
and it died asphyxiated with its head sticking out.

And I called the exterminator who took it upon himself
to lecture me on the life they have beneath the earth
with piles of photophobic, sluggish kids you can see through
who are afraid of going outside, and I was feeling bad
about killing anything which as my mother says "works hard
as a dog," and, besides, I always wanted to pop through too
though I don't sleep, not half as much as my cats do,
and I get mad and walk them around like little o.d. victims,
trying to make them pay attention.

So I told this guy to get under the house and do his thing
but be gentle, and I lay there overwhelmed by the way
the outside world reaches in, the way the life beneath us
reaches up, and mostly how the inner life, which in my case
is a miracle, isn't afraid to stick its neck out.

Hardware

Because I have the money now,
I order in a truckload of nails, cement,
and thousands of feet of gutter.
I help the driver lug them down
to the basement and pay him twice
his weekly salary to go upstairs
and make-believe he's arguing
with customers in broken English.

Everyone's house is falling down.
There's no other store for miles.

I'm in the basement
crawling over nails, stacking
the cement. I swear an oath
to remember all this, the way my hand
dredges bleeding through the keg of nails,
the dead body weight of the cement,
the shriek and blast of the gutters
being dragged and stacked.

Meanwhile the driver has gone crazy
with power and is screaming down the stairs
how I'm no good. I'm fired.
So I give him the finger in the dark
and wish he was dead
like when I was a kid and I hid
between the stacks of cement bags
like a timed explosive
waiting to grow up,

crooning to myself, yeah, yeah,
so this is what it's like.
Only this time I tell myself
I got the money,
and whenever I feel like it
I can get out.

Air Mail Shoes

When I woke today somehow
the birdsongs seemed harder and smaller.
Time much longer than a day must've passed
last night. I live in the belly of an animal
as I always have, but today I sense
the animal has risen or is dead.

I feel calm, like a doctor does
when hysteria breaks into his office
with its limb hanging by a thread
and he smiles reassuringly as a tourniquet
and then bears down.

Have I finally fixed the breath-taking
swirls of cloud-art that wheeled me through
and through me the wind-driven years?

There's no proof that anything's happened,
but look at me being awesome on this inner birthday,
answering the door in my red-striped pajamas
and signing for a Special Delivery package –
my beat-up old shoes which I left at my millionaire
brother's house, who by this small act
                              of extravagance and kindness
has proved he's doing very well.

Well, me too.
In this business of watching everything,
everything happens once and for all.
These shoes are proof.

2

The

Diamond

Explanation

Dazzling and tremendous how quick the sun-rise would kill me,
If I could not now and always send sun-rise out of me.

— Walt Whitman

Mom Did Marilyn, Dad Did Fred

We sat there, her tiny audience,
as she slunk downstairs, poured
into her sparkling blue gown,
kissing the red-hot air and singing
"Diamonds are a girl's best friend"
into each of our little faces
that blushed at how deeply she was
committed to being sexy, and at Dad
suavely twirling her out the house
and down the street in his convertible.

The tunafish sandwiches, the blitzed TV
faded in an obliterating glitter
of glitz and wet kisses, and I
with my face turned toward
the heaven of things I would do someday
made up my mind too soon
to have other notions of beauty.

As Long as You're Happy

— in memory of Ruth Myers

I don't know what the Bible says.
My mother who died after being
mercilessly kept alive
by machines at the hospital
looked at the photo of my fiancée
and said, "As long as you're happy…"
as if it were the final measure of my reach.

The star through which I shot
my young heart has little value now
except as an occasional reference point,
a piece of cosmic punctuation
some third-rate planet may depend on
to survive.

What I thought was an ethical problem
of existence was just a broken heart.
The woman for whom I have ransomed
my wife and children would like to erase
the past. I would like to gather them all,
please, under one roof, one heart.

About my mother…
each day the doctors and machines
said her chances of living
with one more operation
on her overburdened heart
would probably be better.
I thought of reading the Bible then.
It wasn't a question of being happy.

I Will Steal Some for Her from You

The way I hold you for dear life,
entwine your sleep with mine,
is the way my mother's letters say
she's fine and do not mention she is old,
that each eye has revolted from its axis
in her search for what is missing.

Her hug crushes
but cannot touch what's wrong.

I never bought you jewelry
because silver and turquoise spill
from your slightest question,
necklaces of laughter slide from the sides of the bed.
But someone has been paring and slicing,
grating and crumbling my mother's voice.

Whatever she is saying, the noise of miners
is roughing back the edge.

Once she had an assortment of pretty dresses
and men hungry for her. Now she has courage
and grown sons on whom she has worn herself out
like a washrag on the rocks.

Thinking of her stooped over,
I feel the world's been finally cleaned.

I tell you this because nobody has
explained it to me. Who would bother
to explain a letter rising on the wind?
But the hammer falling....
There needs to be an explanation.

Walking, Walking

In the far North
where the eye travels
through six kinds of whiteness
until what it imagines and what it sees
are counted as the same,
there is a hero named
Man-Made-of-Distances.

Except for how he lives out there
past everything
and how far he sees,
he is like my father
disguised by reality
whom I have always strained to see.
But my father remains my father,
invisible arms held out to me.

Someone must've told him who he was
was wrong. He's that uncomfortable.
He's made of distances
and with his departure he takes his absence with him.
He peels the very landscape from the land
and walks off with a wave stuck somewhere
between a hi-sign and a slap.

So Father,
when you open the door of emptiness,
when you turn away,
when you walk toward what others call nothing,
my wish for you is that you see the void,
how it splits itself
as glass splinters light
into its thousand true colors.

Leaving the Light on

Returning home late one night
I realized I had no idea
who Mother and Father were.
So I climbed the spindly apple tree
wondering why darkness made me larger
and peered inside their room
listening first to one,
then the other, like oars
dipping in the darkness
towing the lighted window away.

They were explaining while they spoke
the simple names of things
through which the world fell through
confused: Mother, Father, Home;
offering directions
to each other
like polite strangers,
the ones who go on
when it's all done,
half-finished, just begun,
and they go on.

The Gift

Remember Father's Day, the banner says.
But I can't give my father what he wants
much less name it, so I get him a golf machine
that pops the ball right back.

If I can't give him what he wants
I can get him what seems wrong.
It's the thought that counts, he'd say,
not having caught the exact misses
I sent past him into interstellar space.

I'm telling my wife how she looks super-good
in this flouncy purple maternity suit,
though in truth it looks like her behind
is in front, when I suddenly think
I'm going to be a father! and I remember
my own two kids who don't live with me anymore
and I get quiet in order to receive their thoughts.

But instead I think about these poor Black kids
I took for a ride through White North Dallas
and how one little six-year-old beauty
leaned over my shoulder and shouted to the wind,
"How do you get to live like this?"

Imbalance

Just before leaving her room
I pull the curtains back and reveal
the wheeling universe that falls
over the house and will not stop falling.

She loves in the silent profusion
of young girls giving off the scent
of cinnamon, and busying the air with images
she circles her nipples with her fingertips
then falls asleep.

It's impossible to be accurate
going by the feel of things.
The light of the star she singled out
to make a wish
was extinguished before her birth.

I work best with darkness and this is it,
the dark block of emptiness I live in,
from which no sound or light escapes.

I'm building an æsthetic
based on imbalance
as the Korean potters did
for a small off-kilter work.
It'll complement the earth:
an enormous intention inside a small life.

I wonder what she wished.

Homemade Birthday Gift

You left your crumpled nightgown hanging off the bed
like a piece of the ragged darkness you woke up in,
one sleeve reaching out as if you had sighed
from your open hand. It had that look of grief
only the emptiness of clothes can describe.

I'm stitching night scraps into something suitable.
I'm tearing out the crooked lines.

These are only wild guesses, like the criss-crossed
trails birds leave dissolved against the morning sky.
They fly like you on the needlepoint of instinct
at the sun's first ray, leaving behind that noise
of tearing across the darkness like a present being opened.

The Diamond Explanation

In your braided hair
I have placed a diamond
like the small silence
we undress inside of.

Love's beautiful nail
makes a stunning light remark
about pressure and darkness:
how long it takes, faced with myself,
to break open a little light.

Take this morning. Chained
to my cigarettes, I go toting
the instruments of my habit
thinking nothing of the accumulation
of ashes and smoke, which is
a terrible metaphor for love
that lovers understand.

They know the great thing about being human
is its depth, the thoughtlessness and art
of every gesture, the responsibility
of the still life left behind.

This is why I bought the diamond,
to remind me of the Everlasting
from blown ashes and smoke,
of solitude's wild and quiet transformations
while we're getting dressed.

All I Can Do

If I were a Japanese artist
I'd paint the gleaming faucet
ticking precisely
in front of the wild sunshower
outside our kitchen window.

Instead I sit here quietly
and place your beautiful intensity
against you
as you walk by casually
to do the dishes.

Blue

Today I throw a ladder against the deep blue moment
when something that you do is so beautiful
it opens up a day that hallucinates a deeper blue.

The desire I feel when I'm away from you
is blue imagining itself; yes, imagination's blue.
And the blue when you are near me is the odor of blue,

meaning desire, not for the thought of you, but for you.
Inside desire, which is me feeling everything is blue,
you go from you to blue and I desire you more.

Then a deeper blue comes over me – you. Then your blue,
which is your desire for me, comes over you,
and then comes my blue, re-desiring you, over you.

A Manner of Speaking

My wife exclaimed, "¡Qué macho!
How mature your penmanship is!"

I said, "That is nothing, my bird-like bird,
but why do you speak to me in Spanish?"

"Oh," she said with her little mouth stuck like a cherry tomato,
reminding me of the time she had called me a jeweler with a salad,

"I was to market today and this stallion of a farmer
took me in his arms and sold me muchas penumbras."

"¡Qué Dios, Conchita Estrellita con Quesa!" I explained.
"Do you think it is me when I am not at the market?"

She twirled her entire lovely body around twice and said
in her palest voice, "No, Herbert, my life is the trudging bore
I'm trapped inside. I would soon evaporate in madness
if it weren't for the efficacious power of your vocabulary."

"That is nothing, my flower-like tulip," I said, asking
if we were now in England and by what fortuitous trick
in my expression we had been transported there.

"Mon cher," she whispered, twisting her waist coquettishly,
reminding me of the sensual syntax of Balzac,

"Zee chauffeur took me to a tiny garden on the outskirts
of zee city – très magnifique – and there in your name and honor
praised your incomparable generosity to zee hilt."

"Mon Dieu!" I gasped, "François du Monde du Vichyssoise,
is it me you think I am when I am not in the driver's seat?"

"Ziegfried," she shuddered, "vhen vill you see zee devastating power off your mind on me? Your mere presence eez incredible."

"Zat eez noszing, my doe-like fawn," I laughed, to which she laughed, and then my laughter roiled over hers, and then she cut under mine, and then I tried my lower boiling gutterals, and she careened even higher, and so I could do nothing but enlarge the geography of our joy as she set sail and I watched over her to discover, as it were, the farthest regions of our communal bliss.

The Problem with Love Poems

In the museum there's a statue of an Aztec king
with a big erection. He looks startled,
just staring off in space.

Around him are the masks of demons
which are what he must've been thinking of
as he was being sculpted that moment
into endless time and space.

He seems a flashback and a prophecy
of the shocked moment at school
when I was staring ludely at the beauty
Marylou Mulcahy just as the teacher commanded me
to stand and recite.

The friend I'm with says, "This guy
couldn't of been king of anything
except his own queer dreams."

"Precisely," I say, "I think he *is* adrift
and this is the glorification of The Ephemeral Moment
when The Mystery Of The Ordinary is caught
unconscious and incarnate."

"Yeah," my friend says, looking off in space,
"she must of been great."

Natural Ice Cream

Sometimes when I'm tired of your dark beauty,
my right hand grows enormous,
the tunnel of my eye grows inward,
and I can't bear to eat a piece of fruit.

I love you, I love you, I love you with all my heart,
I say,
driving the car back and forth
over a pomegranate.
The meter is stuck on red.

And now my brain outweighs me,
now I'm tired.
After I clean up the house
I'm gonna put a bullet through my head.

Later on, we can go out someplace nice
for natural ice cream.

Perspective

I am sitting in my chair
in the blue sky
thinking about being pregnant
getting smaller and smaller
condensing into a
little Buddha belly
which will later turn
under my blind right hand
and pull me through again
whatever I've become.

It's fantastic to think
how we're born, one human
pulled out of another
like perspective in a painting
I think
as I recede
in my Chair of Fatherhood.

Once in a while
I go down amid the tumult
of stuffed animals
and tell my wife
who is so lost inside herself
she cannot wake nor sleep
a story. Not a real one
but one in the bright colors
of a daydream
like the one I tell myself,
one that comes alive.

The Discovery of Peanut Butter

The beautiful Juanita hates me today.
A flash of purple and she slipped off to the lagoon.
I shrieked after her like the white cockatoo,
the one who makes the feathers on his head
stand up one by one in a slow wave
like I do when I'm getting a plan.

I am roasting peanuts over a hot pit.

It is like holding moonlight inside the earth
when I make love to Juanita.
But tonight she looks at me as if I tasted awful.

When we were little children
I could always make her happy
by jumping up and down on my food.

The Poet as Househusband

My sad blue crushed velour
is tugging on the line
like a grouper
that's swallowed a whole blue rainy day.
I need to sit down beneath it and strum a guitar.
Why didn't I, like everyone else, ever learn to play guitar?

And you my darling Vice-President of Digital Systems Inc.,
your red Cha-Cha blouse is trilling through its teeth
like Charo — big tush, no talent,
she wants it all this very minute, screaming,
"Weeee! I luf you! Here, I kiss you! Where the party is?"

Next to her my underwear looks bored.
Poor pilgrims, they dream of swallowing oysters,
gulping beer; objectively in love with their life
of dull refusals, in love with being bored.

Darling, everything was excruciating today,
thank-you-very-much.
When you come home you'll find I've fainted.
I left the steak out on the sink to thaw.

Leaves

Sometimes you just want to live in the song itself
so you just sit down.

All those birds going crazy in the trees,
they do it all the time!

Now I suppose someone very learned is going to come
and slow everything down to a noun.

But I like the rule that asks
"What's the greatest song on earth?"

And the trees in the world stand up
and the ramshackled birds of the heart go crazy.

Did I?

You don't take my legs very seriously.
You think I have sincere eyes
which means I can just about
get to you, but no matter how hard
it is getting there, I arrive
at the same time
as your disconcerting smile.

Some people can say, "What impudence!"
"Just who do you think you are!"
and the shape of that sticks perfectly
to their faces like grilled cheese.

My highest achievement is,
"Now just hold on a minute…"
accompanied by my father's squint
and that feeling of snapping backwards.

"What the hell are you talking about?"
you say. I say, "Read my lips: L-E-G-S!"
The other day I opened the door
to take a walk and there was this
velvet rope across the walk
with a sign saying,
"This room is closed. Please be seated."
So I stood there confused by my legs.

I'm talking about my legs metaphysically
and you tell me, "Relax, you have cute legs."
Outside, people are shooting the finger at each other
intuitively all over the place.
They know what's going on.

But when I look into your girlfriend's eyes
slowly and tell her she better leave town
or her heart will be broken,
and I'm dictating straight from the top of my head,
you shoot a look at me and say, "Asshole,
she *is* from out of town."
Well, I didn't day she wasn't, did I?
And I may not have said it then
but I was talking metaphysically.

Black and White

—for my sister, Ellen

All her life
my little sister
wanted a horse.
So I got her one
just like that.

It was black and white,
sort of sad for no reason,
gazing in a field
with no wind around it.

You should've seen her
jumping for joy,
kicking for joy
like a little horse.

Mother said, "You can't
have a horse in the city.
How will you feed it?
Where will it sleep?"

Where will you sleep,
little sister,
waiting for me
to do the magic touch again?

Once in a while
I call her up
and ask how she is.
Sort of sad for no reason.
"Hello." "Goodbye."
That's how it is.

Tribute to Cagney

I'm the kinda guy
who's been in traction all his life,
who cracks his knuckles with a dark remark
then ends up chunking a .45
through his reflection.

I never woke up singing
"God, it's great to be alive,"
the wind tossing its underwear into the trees,
an orchestra of light bouncing off the grass.

So don't be giving me that crap
about feeling good and helping others.
I'm the kinda guy who helps himself.
I may not be the meanest guy in town
but the meanest guy don't fool around with me.

What's your idea of feeling good?

3

The

Diaspora

I sometimes think that never blows so red

— Omar Khayyam

The Diaspora

By what name will they call
the disheveled temple
inside me
except by my name?

In whatever city this is
whoever hears the congregation
of my voices chanting
in a rented room
will be disabled by them.

I keep two immaculate white cats
to restore my memory of tranquility
and I have nailed the people I love
in another life and more and more
the temple is inscribed
in an alphabet of indecipherable
accidents and impressions.

Once I looked up to a God who wore
an expression from a joke
I never quite got. Now I hide my face
in the beauty of my lover
whose cries of pleasure twist shamelessly
like smoke beneath a door.

She tells her father maybe someday
I'll be famous, but he thinks
it is only in the way
someone has perfected a technique
for decanting a dangerous fluid.

She puts the stone I'm curled inside of
in her mouth and speaks about our future

in which I am the distant blueness
and the blown stars of her breath
are lights along our way. I hold onto her
blinded by promises.

After the many deaths and accomplishments,
each man makes an order of his own.
I think this solitude of rock
is a tiny piece of God's great loneliness
in which birds with strings of sunlight
in their beaks fly through. So the saying
of my name makes an order of its own.

Like Trees in the Desert

As if they were planting a garden of flesh
with rulers and sticks and hands and boots
they used to beat us hard in Hebrew School.

We were terrible kids, always raising our hands
to go to the bathroom, please, and always denied.
So once we did it in a paper bag, lit the bag on fire,

and roared when the teacher tried to stamp it out.
They beat us with the literal and we cried out
for God to hold those beatings in His hand and

strike the teacher dead. I always wandered off
in my head trying to figure out just whose body
I was in and what the hell is all this anyway?

I remember nothing of my childhood except its streets
and the way sharp stones jutted out, which means
I must've been looking down a lot. Oh, I remember paying

my dime each week to buy a tree in Israel, leaf by leaf,
to make the desert bloom. And I assume that by now
somewhere in the desert there's a tree representing me.

Biography by Surfaces and Distance

He took the image of himself from coloring books.
Never more than one child at a time, a black line
of simplicity describing absence, inviting someone else
to fill it in:

> He is turning purple
> reaching for a tangled kite.

> He is selling apples
> from a fiery tree.

> He is on a see-saw
> balanced off the page.

> He is chasing a ball
> the color of the world.

He learned to scrape his crayons sideways in a blur,

> laid one color over another
> to create the illusion of depth,
> an impression, in a word.

He kept his water colors hidden.

> Even the simplest feelings bled.
> No matter how he blew and blew
> and turned the landscape sideways,
> it still turned red, like dusk,
> when Mother called him to his chair
> and he filled his absence in.

Later on he dawdled by the restless sea

which had no borders to its immensity
which looked back at him looking
until a line ended the picture
with his wish to be a man.

Finally he turned to mirrors

but couldn't fake himself out.
They held his worst and best
but mostly all the in-betweens
except reversed. Even the colors
which in his mind he knew were real
in real life only seemed.

Not a bad life. It even contained some dreams:

a few books, a half-finished house
in which someone who loved him grieved.

A life matched evenly to others
if you stood far off, detached.

Now, Children, Close Your Books

They have bolted the swivel seats to the floor
and washed out the gaping mouth of the blackboard.

Dust from the moon hangs in the buzzing fluorescence,
the sound of children made to sit still.

The octogenarian crossing guard disappears into the distance
waving his orange flag at death, but only a few cars stop.

Now, Children, open your books
to the page where anything can happen:

if you are X and the dull hours of afternoon light
lifting the building a little bit are Y

and the rank smell of bologna and bread inside your desk
has the power to remind you of arithmetic thirty years later

and all the teachers are old ladies dying
with the names of objects and flowers

and a haunting voice drives through you
and makes up your mind to never return

and that feeling of sacredness you held
like a lucky penny in your hand

you can't name or find or live for anymore —
then, Children, how will you live?

Reunion

I would have planted pansies,
the flowers that dance with each other,
but they reminded me of the '50s, black circles
of badly put on make-up around the girls' eyes,
how they went limp in their stack chairs
after hours of not being asked, went home,
gossiped on the phone about who said what,
their yellow and purple chiffon dresses
foolishly imploding on an empty chair,
the petals of their bouffant hairdos
curled in lumpy rollers, and how hard it was
for us guys to cross the waxed darkness
of this derelict ship webbed with crêpe,
the history of our sadness blooming
under full sail, to ask do you want to dance.

The Town I Came from Never Read a Book

"Hitting [well] doesn't come from how strong you are,
it comes from the heart."
— *Ronnie Lott, San Francisco 49ers*

It's hard to believe
the guys are still standing there
punching each other in the arm.
But that's the punchline,
a wicked hammerlock thrown up
and locked with the epithet
"Smack" or "Duh" and, of course,
the beautiful "Kiss"
who for all her two-faced emptiness
shall remain frozen in this poem
in a mid-air split.

In a rain forest in Honduras
a vine strangles a tree into a twisted mass
known as plum-pudding mahogany
whose "tortured" grain dives deep and back
like rapids of somber light, or pages being flipped
by the bored rich, before it is cut and stacked
in flitches and then fused shining to
the top of an expensive table.

I saw Kiss years later on a TV show.
She was one of two scantily clad girls
on the Pro Golf Tour telling the viewers
what the score was in simple big numbers.
I'll spare you the rest about Smack and Duh
except to say that once upon a time
there were characters in a town
that was like a book made from trees
which were twisted by a certain lack of light
by which nothing could be read.

Self-Defense

Lesson One is the last move,
the breaking of the neck.

Lesson Two breaks down need
into two steps: Bow deeply,
please, to everything dark
that has ever happened to you.
Think of yourself as inept.
Then consider your opponent
dead. This makes the present
so efficient it becomes the past.

Step Two is a clearing of the head:
like a sip of water before wine
or a high-diver who shakes his hands
into being still, you must sing
the song of the future
out of which you will step
allowing it to join the past.

Lesson Three will take years.
You must learn to wait.
There will always be someone coming at you
from an unexpected direction; he is
to be expected. You must carry with you
a feeling of success.
This is the weapon you'll conceal.
It is, I think, how a flower must feel

just before it blooms. Only here we are
speaking of death.

Some of you will misconstrue the object
of self-defense, will, out of pride,
reverse the lesson so you become
the victim. This brings me to
the philosophy of violence,
the meaning of self-defense.

Once

Once I would've given anything to live in the desert.
I could've lived on dew and the great chord of silence
throbbing in the undulating heat. I could've composed
under the light of my own star.

I planned to work my way across on Uncle's ship
but my own blood let me down. He told my mother,
who gave me this worried life. In those days
I couldn't get around her. I never got across.

By now I have a face of rock and no one alive to stop me.
But I think those years of deserts and seas are all
inside me. So there's no use going now,
no use pulling against the blood.

Most of Us

In another age I would've married a sorry woman
from my small village, had too many children,
broken my back with my hands, and come home drunk.

I would've died early from diseases, having suffered
humiliation after humiliation, my heart twisting at the sight
of a coin, while our hated king lived far off on a hill.

I would've believed in anything that was given,
been on my knees to anything with a singular face.
I would not have been as I am, one who believes in himself

and nothing else, to whom everything else is in service,
and live up here in a bewilderment of choices,
doing what I choose, The King of Everything.

The Waiters

Half-drunk with beautiful women
I live like a king who suffers
bad dreams he cannot remember
or interpret: someone is quietly
laying down dishes of Chinese food —
scallions, carrots, hot spiced meats.

After a while I tell the story again
and, as usual, no one knows how to respond.
I notice how everyone thinks of picking
something difficult to get onto his fork —
slivers of snow peas, slices of bamboo shoots.

I tell the old story of waiting and grief,
coming out of nowhere, that everyone knows.
I haphazardly change every detail
but it becomes more universal.
It begins to make more sense.

Then things get serious and we talk
like lonely children about lost chances
and broken resolutions as the piles of food
glaze and slump over the plates —
cashew chicken, mounds of pearly shrimp.

The noise of the other patrons blurs
into an animal happiness as we seem
to fall asleep staring at a grain of rice.
Then the waiter reappears with cookies
mildly curled and folded over, asleep.

Finally, we break the cookies open
and settle on some distant good news.
I look far away as if I had remembered
something important. But it is nothing,
nothing. The waiters who have seen it all before
stand unnoticed and attentive at the doors.

The New Feeling

Lately I've had this permanent feeling of falling.
Concentrating on this takes all my time,
so I've become an expert at the instant getaway,
the one-liner: "Excuse me," I say, "I'm falling."

I'm not falling because something bad once happened
and I'm not disappointed or bitter.
As naturally as blood rains down in me
I fall like a closed umbrella.

No one notices this in me and no one ever said, "Look,
this strange thing will happen one day." So it must be
everyone's falling, only no one's saying a word.

Once I saw this movie about a woman obsessed
with dancing who wore these great red shoes.
Whenever she put them on, she leaped and lurched and
twirled and finally got crushed by a train.

That meant something to me and for thirty years I thought
it was my own queer dream. Then I discovered everyone
had seen the movie, only no one was saying a word.

Well, this time I'm saying it first.
I'm calling it as I feel it.
It isn't love and it isn't death.
I'm talking about falling.

Well

I have tried to do one thing well
without resources. And I've never been any place
foreign. When I address myself I feel
pressed to death by the need to sleep,
like those public situations in which I scatter
into the nearest molecules whose alarms
start ringing so loudly that the dinging makes
the intervals of silence sound like ball bearings.
Only I look normal and people think I'm nice.

Has anyone ever heard or read about being sick
as the one thing one does well?

When I put my head down where my head has been
I smell my sleep and sleep. That's when the feeling
of being drained away leaves me intact and I arise
refreshed as a cold balloon ride heading toward
the obliterating buckshot of right now.

Okay, I think we're ready to order now, please.
We'll have a #6, a quietly uplifting image of nature;
and a 21, a smart summarial remark; and I guess
we'll have a #37, an inconspicuous mental breakthrough.

What I mean by *well* is like those tags on damaged goods
that say "as is" as "as is" is, not like might have been,
which is irrelevant, yellow sign, beside the point,
hard hats only, out-of-the-question, unsafe at any speed,
which is me falling down on myself per second squared
onto the plaza of another public situation.

The Mind's Voice

It's incredible how it just goes on and on
out of control like some half-mad relative calling
on the phone to report an imagined slight, the most
appropriate gift, the same old gnawing on the same old bone.

And the sound we hear — androgenous and black —
as if transmitted from a hole whose pull
stripped the voice of its human characteristics
into something half-electrical, small, and cracked.

And we never quite hear it right.
Like a floater in the eye that sails from our attention,
it drifts beyond our words, like Grandmother droning on
with her mouth full of stories about the Old Country.

At night the mind foams over the edge of sleep
and rains down in countries where emotions grow
larger than trees, where rapid eye movements climb
for their lives out of this dream until we hear a dot

splash down somewhere in a distant sea. Then it leaves
the glassy-eyed surface healed. "Good mornink...," says
Grandmother, calling us down in that voice that tells us
stories of ourselves in a mouth full of broken English.

Dried by Darkness

I am hanging clothes in a solar eclipse,
black sun like the confusion in emergéncies
when a blue party dress turns black,
a white silk blouse burns like remembrance,
and birds return to their trees shamed
by squabbling when the world is about to end.

Something like an inconsolable mind of sadness
passes across an object, and the shadow
of an open door rises up, swallows the house,
and continues rising into the larger darkness
that is everywhere and makes things nothing
and balls its stillness into the sense that
this is what we're waiting for.

All my life I've been warned
not to look directly at this light.
So I make a pinhole of desire
on a blank piece of paper
as if proof were needed
to see the light being eaten away,
as if proof were needed
that something being erased
in this life
could burn out my sight.

The Reason Why

Since I have an affinity
for silence and vacuums,
I figure I was bitten by the moon.

The way I've gotten dreamy, fat, and bald,
there's a reason for it now.

Look at the slow roll and drift
of that stupid face
lit against all that darkness.
It makes perfect sense!

Contributor's Note

I am brushing what's left of my hair
beautifully, slowly
in honor of the year I froze in an unheated warehouse
and for my dog, Sam, who couldn't take it and took off.

While my father explained what I looked like
with the question, "How can you live like this?"
I thought the hard facts of life would build character.
I was in the big city on manuevers, going through myself like war.

I am taking my time deciding which arm
should go into my worn shirt first
in memory of the people I squandered
with my eyes shut
to whom, for whatever kept them with me, I apologize,
and who, for whatever they saw in me that was good,
couldn't possibly know the vanishing point I believed in,
that there would hardly be room for myself.

In the old days I couldn't possibly make a mistake:
the cold, the hunger, the twisted nightpeople,
the useless jobs in back rooms, basements, laboratories,
high-rise cubicles, dizzying ledges, open sea, lonely cab,
looking in the mouth of kegs of nails, the human brain,
shark guts, mock-ups; from a ten-story scaffold
to my tent on Bolinas Mesa, I look back
out of broken back and bridgework at the incredibly open
face in my high school yearbook which quotes me as saying,
"Do your best."

And it has come to this taking my time
to get ready, this stuffing my blood
with corsages of debris and neglect.
I am washing my face slowly because
the ceremony of slow deciding is itself
getting ready, and taking my time means
I am not ready, go on without me,
I am not ready yet.

Secondhand Pleasure

And this reading of the burning paper is the answer given
to the primary enthusiasm of the poet, which is nothing less
than to bring life into the being of one who hears him.
— Vicente Aleixandre

Here I am in the poetry section
craning my neck
in a half-priced bookstore
screaming to myself,
"This guy's no good!"
"Here's a first edition!"
my foot on my pile of books
as if some poetry thug
might mug me.

I'm drilling through
with the light in my head
when that look of bone
and weight of resignation
that old books have
impress on me how all the joy
and fever ends up dumped down here.

And then there it is —
I'm clobbered!
There's my own first book
and inside I'm bent over
a cup of coffee
scribbling notes
on a napkin at 3 a.m.
in Bickford's Cafeteria
while my father cruises by

not wanting to intrude
as he waited for me
to finish 100,000 cups
of steaming black thinking.

He didn't know
the waitress there
knew Yeats by heart
and would be off work soon
or that we'd end up married
then divorced. I didn't know
his sadness.

I just wanted to save my book
which I held for a while
like a child struck down
in an argument with someone else.
It takes a long time
for a thinking man
to decide
not to do anything,
to put the book back on the shelf
and just walk out
worried and confused
but doing alright.

Cross Country

I never woke you as we drove across
the Great Plains in the high darkness
trying to reach the Mississippi, me
listening so hard to a small metallic noise
inside the engine's roar that it seemed quiet
as I drove on tense, exhausted, undecided,
until you woke and heard me say go back to sleep.

I can still hear you shout "Get out!"
as the wheels fell off our marriage
and our son, sobbing and hugging our knees,
tried holding us together. Sometimes when I call
I close my eyes and follow that line
flying through the darkness like a Roman candle
ending in a burst of darkness and ringing,
and my own small voice out there on its own
comes back at me, asking hello, who is this, hello?

Waiting for the Part with a Bite Out of Me to Snap

I was used to hearing my neighbors cursing "Christ!"
and the walls of my house so thin
I thought someone's calling me
and I'd get up and say
"Okay, I'll fix it." And I'd end up
with my head inside the "everything drawer"
looking for my goddamned melted hammer
so I could whack what was wrong back in place.
And when I fixed it so it didn't move
I'd say to myself like a one-trick dog,
"Pretty Good, have a beer."

In those days it was almost always winter
and the sweet old hungers drove me inward
and I'd trudge upstairs and pull the chain
to light the darkness up, and then I'd write
while the vines grew crazily across the window
and the cats sat waiting to beam me down.

In those days everything was going to happen
because I said so, and a promise was a promise,
because I knew I knew a few things deep enough
so when I'd say these things I'd never blink:
"Once and for all, this is for keeps."

And eventually I got across. Everything's finally fixed.
I've got a garden full of pecans and plums and a skyful
of passing pleasantries. Lying here, I imagine painting
a courtesan in a purple sari through which the afternoon light

is shining. And she, feeding me fruits and nuts, is giving
herself to me bit by bit under the guardian trees
against a harmony of blue.

But then there's the feeling of a specific lack of depth
and I suggest right out of the blue there should be
a strike force of stony black birds
diving diagonally down.

Inducement

Having nothing or
not knowing what to say
he dropped a grain of sand
into his eye
which slammed shut
and watered.

The other eye, still open,
registered nothing or
rather the blizzard
of nothing and, of course,
watered like an infant bawling
in a roomful of other infants bawling
unappeasably just because.

So there arose a great unhappiness
and this is the story that goes along
like when you're on a train
that begins to move and you think
it's the landscape moving
this is the story that goes along
to make things better
because someone cried out
something large and invisible
has been passed down
out loud in secret.